FREE VERSE EDITIONS

Edited by Jon Thompson

CHILD IN THE ROAD

CINDY SAVETT

For Jim + Judith —
Best —
Cindy

Parlor Press
West Lafayette, Indiana
www.parlorpress.com

Parlor Press LLC, West Lafayette, Indiana 47906

Printed in the United States of America
S A N: 2 5 4 - 8 8 7 9

Library of Congress Cataloging-in-Publication Data

Savett, Cindy, 1953-
  Child in the road / Cindy Savett.
    p. cm. -- (Free verse editions)
  ISBN 978-1-60235-029-8 (pbk. : alk. paper) -- ISBN
978-1-60235-031-1 (hardcover : alk. paper) -- ISBN 978-1-
60235-030-4 (adobe ebook)
  I. Title.
  PS3619.A85C47 2007
  811'.6--dc22

                                    2007037865

Printed on acid-free paper.
Cover photograph: "Walking Away Girl" © 2007 by
Olga Sapegina. Used by permission.

Parlor Press, LLC is an independent publisher of scholarly and
trade titles in print and multimedia formats. This book is available
in paper, cloth and Adobe eBook formats from Parlor Press on
the World Wide Web at http://www.parlorpress.com or through
online and brick-and-mortar bookstores. For submission
information or to find out about Parlor Press publications, write
to Parlor Press, 816 Robinson St., West Lafayette, Indiana,
47906, or e-mail editor@parlorpress.com.

for Rachel

July 19, 1991 – May 26, 2000

CONTENTS

ACKNOWLEDGMENTS

Poems from *Child in the Road* have appeared in *Margie, Heliotrope, Diner, LIT, The Marlboro Review, 26 Magazine, CAB/NET,* and *tinysides*.

CHILD IN THE ROAD

I

ALIBIS

I am sorry for the cradle
the walk   between dreams

for the distance ignited
in your eyes

I count
seeds from wavering dogwoods

collect white knives
from your mouth

———————————

of soft death
the assault and the still place

blessings   dark from the middle song
of roiling waters between my teeth

night ruminations
of an oak trunk and the overgrown thunder

a turn of justice in the branches
small forecast in single flight
          a flash of gold

of lost water   and the wreckage

my honey breath
lies in the shelter of your bones
soiled

by the sounds of the dead
that caravan beneath my feet

I am tethered by alibis of blue air

volumes of silence catch in my voice

    signet of the forgotten
    and the listed dead

Motherchild
I stroke this day

speak the dance
of a closed leaf
       jawed by the wind

incarnate the language
for heavy
light

buried in the white day
on unwatered
seed

mistaking
your bloodied arms
for a random touch   or dark songs
for the white of your trill

and bare   stripped   stalk
with nothing but the bone
and the wind
wet through your words.

Begin in the stick time

I am dust
faceless
the wicked sands   and the waters that caress the sky

air
caught
in the turning grains

I am the book of winds
the red dew
petals across my chest

I am the chaste   night   mountain
a coiled wind
exhaling
shadows of crystalline black

I am the mouth of Great Blue Breath
a bare scent
on parched earth

the ribbon of rising wing
kiss of god
          broken
in your pale
eyes

slip into the fire's mouth
with bells around your neck

unknot the ribbons
silk spun of stilled song
        stems curled
        intent on splitting the nightseams

in this theater of roses

I am covered by my nakedness
terrible living of the day

from the underbrush
a hesitancy
pours

one step beating lights below this platform

I dance through an unhinged night
where the breaking occurs

dread in the aborted word

mouth
with a slate tongue

shard
for the master of bared faces

nameless
you have pinned your burnt lips to the morning inscription
                                        spilt vowels from pigeon wings
                        fractured

and come home with salt and blood thread
from the absence

––––––––––––––––

I close the gate to my children
their stomping   and blessing

latch on shattered glass

whisper   red mornings

cast stones in ash
coiled and glazed at my feet

bridge voices in the water

I am your dark
kiss

the creation
of seas   where the dead
float
upright
tilted mouths to scream

the winter grave
of night   swinging   through your hands

an unmarked
heredity of the hard-thrown flood
              the absence of origin

lone player

singing on the trumpet's edge
beside my night
to hone the winter prayer

what was between us

was a demand for names
when the warmth of blood

of wild dogs

was the dream of a dance
with sirens   heavens
and the clotted leaves

and the clearing
mutations
between my fingers

over and over
hands red in repentance

tonight's wings
are blue
first among voices
hovering by the night stalk

meager boundary
between us
      stamp of the foot
      and here I lie

thick dust and the night rhymes

in the ruins of each
spitting tongue

    —————————————

parched accent of the hard dirt

      were you to believe
      in junction   of light then
      I would die

the thousandth time

along the way   I dropped you
and you lay
apart   from creation

midday sun

severs
my tongue

you reach to the birthplace
of gods

along   the way

I have misplaced you among red tulips and the mist

surrendered dayfall
to white breath

ritual of circles
I hollow your name
above faces in the stones and dirt

      blood-drops
near the open cage

————————————

snow harvest

my arms
know you

gray stars
frail hand of god

on the buried
cup

in this terrible
chair
          my summer hands
          touch your lips

abide the early fog

wasp without
her nest

ferry
of death

——————————————

I dig in the ruins
for absence

ignite your canceled breath

again
I have forgotten
your face   a mask of the wary night

               in millions
               of grains
               of sand

II

THE SIFTER

Daybreak haunts
across from where the shining lies

casting
on watersand
canvases of block and paint

swearing away the memory of early dusk

resonant blue
element of the dark

I beat the steel frame

_____

gate unlatched
I exist for the breath-pause
dug-down words of the dark

for the doors that crack
when the keys
splatter   in porous wind

_____

I cover myself in blue
night   endless call
to my bones

I lay by the fire stone
hide the unburied dead

in my throat shrieks the beast

the shuttered dark
flees behind my back

I am the sifter of soundless

                    echoes

        brushed with dirt

and crumbling

      bits of names that stuff my mouth that wound
      my tongue on the falling

scent of sky

edging   towards the blue

I set the night against
my ribs

tilt of heavy
rain
on a vacant yard

(breath consumed)

and wait for the field to answer

settled among leaves
the invisible
hand   cradles   my mouth

Who placates the insistent sand

throatcurves
drawn by the seas
colored glass

Who shadows the undertow

I have fallen from my land
        my host   the throttled clouds
        beading above my lips

——————————————

my tongue spills
salt from the breath
of each day

my voice hollows
the promise   and my recovery

silent white
crowds my mind

whitesilent
day

be servitude
the daily insistent the knitted brow

be the remedy   ignorant in dark gray

be a song through empty bones
         Queen of Mercy
wall that names the dead

coil reins at your feet
malcontent at the blade

broken lock or the key that takes shadow

                    blood drapes the driven light
                    from your knotted
                    wrist

you cull the dark
with the names of birds

    taste salt
    for the meal with the dead

we swing shovels over our heads

calm darkness

————————————

wood in stilled water

drifter
embrace the wooded
peaks of night

insolent dark
hovering at the back
of the neck

III

ALONE AT THE CLAY TABLE

I drown by the roots of the fir
bright space   and the dread

        grave sky
        alone at the clay table

voices hunger in the night language
of water and black wind

wings across each red shoulder
an arrangement of lilies and gold

and the day's long
thrust
into this room of sparrows

————————————

on a palette's disorder
colonies of light
trip
against a river's crossing
shadow

        evening dripping from your palm
        shatters to the ground

Murmur Rachel
sweep of dust across the brow

woman in clover
sews
rabbits to the stems

I   momentary
in an unmarked grove

replicate
the moans

settle the dialogue
        tapping foot
      buried
      by my bedside

frozen
red

_____

thieves of the world's glory
                my hands
                        hover

entwined in ropes among the ruins

my holy
haunted

chained
to broken windows in the tunnel

night patch of loneliness
the initial rhyme

a ruin from the blaze

gold bells and winters breath
score your name

I convert the dead for the ease of translation

shadow of the runaway
spins in the wind

the clanging of sand through my fingers

the day's red
rhythms intend the sunrise
> bring fever to your lips
> fever to my eyes

mix white and silence
with each strike
of the bell

cross shadows of green
and corners of the wind

I hear you   in the nightwebs

—————————————————

shovels by each window   weep

thorns
stumble from your shoulder

I slip through portals
in the silver night

and promise you
silence

I wander in dim light
exposing my shame
at your door

basket of your nighthanging breath
disrupts the evening
tide

I invert your prayers
a decayed religion
by your bed

I free slaves
of Fire   in my breast

———————————

your soul flies from the earth to my mouth

summer leaves and heavy branches
burden the ground

I am the beast
contained

      the prayer shawl of darkness

I heave your plate to the sky

explode
   thousands of crystals in the wind

your name rolls
loosely
in my mouth

crumpled winds
draw your shadow on the glass edge

    sever the tongue
    from your soul

I come by your door
for the bone
for spilt water and muddied words

crier for carrion along this dirt road

―――――――――――

I run fingers across your mouth
where the wind has been

your voice haunts my tongue

the taste of your gaze
shadows my eyes

I wash your body a second time

      my knife is sharp

I am the rain
divider

flames in my clenched mouth

    broken visitor
    at my door

whose crumbling eyes
expunge the blessing

    compass of dread
    crosses my table
    with despair

I sail the shadows
between black pots and covered roots

unearth
keys by each door

the compromise quivers

and remnants of the soiled sun
rest   on my shoulder

drift of crumbling psalms

I ease the way on this knife edge
into the embers of morning

outlined against the stark light
I sing by my grave

standing firm on the water
I sink

---

black seed   I speak the dark

                    and fear aspens marbled whispers that web the sky

silk coins   for the certain hour

---

the rolling pleas
of sweet water songs

          a night   lost to the taste of noon
                    keys lost to the fraught day

only the god's recollection of the ignited hour

tonal prayer of the wind
            lashing
stone
against my face
white and the washing of lips

with blood spots
                    lesions
in a wind stream
secrets of a white sky   and my palms
        drum stories to sudden embers

echo
my silent conference
and curve a finger on the hedge gate
        conform cloudwings to light

deranged days of borrowed red

forgive the fire that scorches the stunned blade of grass
the high strung oak leaf

breath that sears the night
cuts sky to hang across the windows
to bind eyes
shut against the whirling
          of shoulders and arms
          and hips and thighs
and feet wrapped together

and lips   shadows
between the palms

containers
of holes collected by the sightless
for the bone redeemers
          honing a day from midnight air

their bamboo fingers
in the sun

near the roar of ivy
        in prayers and breaking words

and a blue renaissance
seeds   graft to a sanctified sky

eyes surrender   to white air
engage the wind
        speak in waves and paper

tears in the holes of the heart
the eyes
sewn
shut

and the day
a frenzy of swallows
                and sound   witness of flame
                                in the tall grasses

and the living done quickly
exposed sands   in the fingers
of a darkening bay

IV

PURE WHITE

in the faraway   the bamboo
the beginning fence and choking collars
of light
      a sliver of wood beads

and the light vessel
burrowed in dirt

an unfounding of matter
                    a settling of the wide night whispers

fabrics of detonating words
of the scent from moist bones

drifting from beneath the fence

a wicker basket in your arms
for the nightshine
buds

Silence collects
hands
from the blind
        who whisper allnames
                bury the souls of shadows with shovel and dirt

holes of the heart
my blessing

your night   black with holiness

begin with the crossing
stories
and fields of heaven

taste the silence
salt   on a long whistle
smell winds of the darkness

open the night by its winged hinges
frail intention of the blessing on your forehead

the nightmare
coursing
down
your back

for the breath I bred for you

bring your
bones
to the edge of black prayers

and in memory villages
where weeping runs down the walls
I call
your name   to still the sky

tongues
borne by the fired earth

echo the deaf / refused

the tangled earth

————————————

black moon
of a thousand throat paws

to stroke red wolves

bare this
sway
of wild cypress
foot gut
to the grave

and wolf-paws and rain-wails

over earth
all prints for the wild wet

night rage in the coals
and leaves
      breath-weeds of the tongue
          slipping light on the evening descent

and the dark speech
of roots
captured
in a night basket
abrades the day

edits the broken
birth
of white
prayer feet on a dirt
path

———————————

black river road

dirt air
ignites in the palms

hangs low
in gray

shrieks
for reverie
undone in a night's red touch

a gray moon
in the mire

over and over   the dead
devour
the dead sky

worn by rain and the crash of thick dirt
      the dead lay
         flowers with hands   hands
                                from the grave

fractured   torn   bloodied
collisions with stone

———————————

She sweeps the dirt
with blessings
She is the dead one

who climbs night branches
to scratch the wind to weeping
who circles dreamhands

hidden roots She sleeps within
cut and judged
in a clipped dark breath

weave scarlet and fire
through the lips of night

seal the dawn in my throat

strike the open wound
with a bamboo stalk

scour my mouth
to find

the missing deed
sequel   to the forgiveness of red

———————————

construct the breath-lie
from corners
of your eyes

     a single
          refusal of light

in the shade of granite despair

     fire the ovens
     carve holes in your chest
pour burning air to soothe the sores

tie my feet to the wind
bind my tongue
    to drifting light

my eyes become your compass

blood   the paste for your
wings of air and gold

tethered to the bottom stair
my name weakens among stones

in your mouth is a key
dirt and shadow
crowd sounds from the red clay

———————————

pound the night
with your prayer of deliverance

cloak the air with your palms
of shame

light   shadows across your tongue

god of this wasteland
crowned with night
bones

you are glorious
amid the shattered
debris

beneath the freeze

you are the warrior
unhinged traveler
without an oasis of light

you wander
in the commerce of heavy smoke and dried language
need the muzzle   of intent

requiem in the night
asylum

———————————

crawl
echo in the dirt

whose eye burns
through rock

touch nothing

dust in the silent
hour

the hunted
the darkwatch collision with black endings

a circumference of the forest light
        and the flood

uncertain gathering in the center of time
abundant night
falling from an open mouth

each rising word
a latch
on your horizon

———————————

drawn
light

a warwind
in the night's request
for dominion

pure white   the conversation

of doubt

face of the dark green day

you sift the darkness through white teeth
stand
beside fences

where whispers
are the oars in the accident
of birth

god of splintered
light
rises opaque

an ancient bell
loose in the wind

deaf
to the infants and the dying

the quiet
cold in the night

Cancel the moon its singularity
the sun   its collection of stars blue lungs

Cancel the field
landing of sparrows

Roll a game on the sky table
when the dark whirls
or the pen drops twice below the line

Etch scenes of uprising
on my breast

Shame the dreamer
who shakes dandelion manes
in haste for the seeds light lips

assume the tops of trees
are vacant
and blind to frost on the wheat fields

their trunks a gray
darkness
in the wash of yellow and browning earth

that when the crow arrives
and the hawk flies boundaries
in the circle

intent falls
free of the stones
feet pull quickly from the embers

and in the winds exhaust
the journey turns
to will in the fissures of the sun

forgives the messenger
of vacant vowels
a kiss of palms in the black rain

V

YOU

Your name is the ocean reefs
and cliffs of white froth
skies that dip the night to its knees

You are the windcry among tall firs
hands that part seas
in the arc of stars

God of sediment slipping to the sea
child whose feet are darkness
flesh of the coming storm and sand between the lips

You are a single beating wing
a rock split for birthmilk
from under the sifted dirt

come darling
spread your vowels against the wind
a restored feast

fill my glass with the souls of prayers

wrap me in your shawl of
scents

I have chosen dark blue for my breast cover
my mouth skims the body of grace

raw flower of shadow in distant white

VI

THE BLUE NAME RACHEL

while
you sleep

you slip to the shaded
earth

I cover you with my wings
devour
you

your juices soak
my tongue

I rest
on the sun

———————————

in the pit sits the weeper

wrested bones
flee from her hands

bells in her torn
eyes   seal
            the night

I call from under the earth
held in the broad stir
       an uneasy calibration

You enunciate the tremble
            scale clear light

I am the air
by twists and undertones

a forgotten   breath of stone

---

stagger
Wild Moon

shiver dust
      shatter the glass
      mouths of heaven

                birth drunk

mourner
who nurses her dead on maple root
and hungered moss

wild-beats   in a basin of dark

tales of tall men   litany
dribbling from their lips
          and sand
          creeping in crevices of their souls

who is your god

air and thrown clay
          under the sleepers bridge

words spill from your eye
beaten raw by   broom
shovel   hatchet   gun

sail the glance
of blue sun
through dawn rifts

dock the red
to stains of delusion

tether the core
by shattering distance

       light broken
       by a touch
       of pines

       a shift
       in the insistent
       orange

what do I know

light at the edges
reins of earth
a river   of relentless fire

hurl an arrow
through the hunter's word
whispers a moment
                    before a moment after
your scattered flesh
hollows
the wind

slave to my blood
                         with careless fingers
I shovel the Name
from your soiled mouth

that you were me
burns
        through the blue night

you estimate the light
in pieces of debris
        hanging from my fingers

my eyes to the ground

the answer
is where the short night
falls
        and darkness begins
        in spurned reds

the ragged lines of my mouth

I retrieve
your name

secure your arms with twine
against the oncoming dark
        and the slight mistake of the curve

I hold your wrist against
the wind
            bones and ash

you are flying
silence
the mirrored oars of breath in white air

dirt
vines
fire   at my feet

thrashing knot
the smallest light   in my palm

———————————

you   sold in the dark
and I am renamed
Desert

scrape of glass
          rakes
                    through the eyelight
splays lightened dead

arid moon
arcs and you
are the correct shadow

still light mouth
pressed against my dried eye

you recoil   from the uneven might
                    of the dark

the night's breath of cold
astonishment

you summon me to a blue world

a marled configuration
of the righteous iris   the bold rose

your face is at war with the mutinous
stars

———————————

thorns burning
over the backyard fence

a dense percussion of time in the woods

you are the blue wind
a stranger's   pause by the gate

I hold midnight down
with a knife

bleed rain
from tongues

and blacken
breeds
of the earth

do not say my name

———————————

monuments
in my mouth

from the careless of
my breed

            unopened
            bottles
            of vowels

death you hang

the night
blade

    carve fields for Hawk
    archive
    the flight of Great Horned Owl

you hang Mockingbird feet
on the grave

    ——————————

intricate eye

found in glass birds
the feet of dead fish

the white sky
thudding
on the roof

your name

there is no god
no one to seal your lips

no one to anoint your palm
with a kiss

for the footstep
and residence of light
are gone

your vowels
spent
in the trembling

the covenant
breathes of violation

damns
your ladder
built to bear the winds

a fall from the night roof

through the glass terrace
to the pavement glare

have you seen the Sun
in a night terror
when blackness needs a partner
        when bright fire
        whimpers for rain

in the accidental hour
gray doves
peck color from clay

for the words
of a lost child   at the attic door

        bag of salt in her right palm

suck the marrow from my left foot
Freedom Mother
smash faith against the wind

and crawl deep into corners
of carcass craving
mess of wings
in the pit

steaming bowls
stuffed with dark
odor
rotted leaves
descending

shattered
blood tubes
cluttering the lab

bless this plate of bones
bless this twisted flight
this first of hours

bless this carrying horse
knees bent
on Mother's Trail

gods
lost

reduced to breath's insinuation

               fur bristling claws extended
           wings outstretched teeth bared
      tongues hissing quills sharpened

is the blue name Rachel

strong hands of the wind's rope
around a neck

               slipping mist off the lips of the sky

———————————

streamers   from a web

glass
wings

      my vision's blurred

the child's final
words
burn white

on eyelids of the blind

VII

BASKET OF KNIVES

god
who holds angels by the wrists

and tangles
their words in the hair of mourners

open the vault that contains you

illumine
childrens eyes

destroy
    the heavens to unleash you

I am your face   tent in the dark land

wail of the gravemaster

stilled
on your cut lip

               for the winter chill

              for quiet   stone

casket ropes tied to the rising eyes
        and a bucket of honey
        for the wind in my hands

for the planting   forgive me

---

from the stiff bough of a pine tree
the remains of your whisper
chill
early air
      shadow the sky
      in rows of gray

I am a piercing cry

moon   between wingblades
moss in the dark
mouth of eternally   burning   flesh

rustle of water grass
covers my ears

hardened green
notes on each yellowed leaf

my knife has no echo
in ruins of the day

―――――――――

red edge
races the blade
seals veins of dreams

the other name
chews the wind
in my velvet mouth

―――――――――

black breath

wings
and keys

deadly prayer of Names
on my tongue

comfort me

bound to a stone
mask
Dark Heaven

hollow of the knot
        white wings pumping through my veins

cauterize the morning-trap
in my hands

———————————

meal for the dead
white berries
on my
lips

the redundant night
and the moon reflecting night winds

basket of kisses
basket of knives

———————————

burnt wind
kneel

      lash at
blinded bone
wailing
bone

dress the night in jagged glass
                            black monkey

and color dirt shadows
hiding the poet of the blind   poet of the dead
                    in a cacophony of breath

in hollows and fortunes
swallowed by clay and rusted branches

by the throat's desire
acrobat of light

below the bridge
my eyes work the anxious day
to still

      I stammer
      with intent

ghost totem
on my back

nameplates
down this windowless hall

your
breath

————————————

I replant
god
by the fence

the unseen light

and your face in   broken   glass

lullabies from the dirt

the tattered
edge
            between the decibels

be
still

on your head the crown of ferocity

I rock the lungs of a breath abandoned
            inhalations on the curve

————————————

cities breed by my bed
I am the container of still

I am the bowl in descent
knots   behind the wall

moon dripping
through the ends of water prayers

birches in an echo of a yellow voice

In the weapons cave
I can not hear your name

———————————

I touch
your forehead

your overcast
remembrances

code breath
white
on a compass

a survivor's
earthly light

———————————

child in the road
do not go with the smell of death

insist on the unseen day

I fear you
remnant of fire

leakage from the earth

I wait
by my long fence

force the night on its heels
embryo of death

cross a long-plundered
path that circles my home

I engrave your coveted
name by my bed
I assault my face   the unnamed witness

come with me while the night sleeps
and I will buy
your hands from slavery

a stream
of raucous shadows
float the darkness

pitch of dying wolves

caught
by the beast

you toss aside stones

---

underbelly of the morning

do not only begin
with the O

white slope
of the naked earth
disquiet

holy earth
whole dirt

near the original days

I am the blood of a child

the weight of a thread
under the mist

my face is hidden among thorns
   gray drippings from god

       salt tiles
       rage white on my tongue

exhumed by the wind
all the bones of eternity align fevers and sores
with the wooden gate

in the blue breath
I sleep

stars from a wooden rod
for you
who sits in the dark
breeds the night air
          to stream
          the shadow of fallen
          wood

I write your name across my chest
in iron leaves and fire

sand-bricks
dissolve
in my mouth

——————————

I unravel in the night   and do not know my name

by threads you unleash
angels at the water's edge

the wind catches my tongue
I fly off the roof

and find your mouth
with the dark

in the wild dance she is queen

the memory and the mist
a white dream upon her lips

scrim of leaves above her head
vines and the sky terrain

she sorts the rainfall and rotting words
through a veil of ten thousand screams

filters the prayer

VIII

THIS STEP BY THE DOOR

grieve for me
porous light
            wing

I am cousin to the night
with mighty hands that mold
stars from the crumbling
dust of death

high pitch name
struck by tongues
sinking
in the dirt

———————————

shards
and tongues of chance

one hand scars
clay and story

bleeds the seams of night

aroused voices   drip   from the sea
to common ground

       vessels
       of singleminded air

and speak
for the tainted washed ashore

a shine transgressed
by the earth's edges

your flat
mouth
dissolves   in your hands

—————————————

greenwood
listen

for loose rocks
       whitened

and candor fled
for breath wedged
       between black reins

and froth and seethe

flicker and the jousting intend the night
thread gold through my eyes

I cry for your words to enter me

        clamored dirt

disclaimer that wrings seeds
from the vines

the air stills

windows
close

———————————

for light reversed
      by winter's broken moon

chilled
night

      bow down for the naked

giant pines
that howl

you are redeemed

I sweep bushes for sons and daughters
      and find my bones in their feet

counterfeiter of names
   for your tongue   stitched in gold whorls

     and the house in the fire

I bring a basket of bread
bloodwashed at my morning table

              derelict witness to fraying
      light

the brink of your breath

light sways
   yellow on my night wings
crossing branches
to earth

you are a palette of screams
vibrations of the night stride

I am the edges
hum
the rustle
  of wind
between my tongues

I test the night
by descent
  rhythms of shine

you blanket the leaf bed

windows in the silence

distraction   by the moon
assassin of the deep light

a failing in low wind

scoring walls
with sentences and blood
and the patience of each thread in the wearing

of each green blade interned
caution on the pasture

breath comes from eyes that attend
the astonished night

veins
that name light
a call from tall grass
    chords breaching the dark

swift fingers
circling water through the lost book
inviting anonymity on unlined pages
    beneath the soil

———————————

cedars
dropped in the snow

pennies owed
and gold in the grave

seed
the frost

day froth
in the sand blood

and the hourglass calls
avoid minerals of light

gravel and the unswept dirt

    in that pause an alignment
    of pebbles
    brief persuasion of time

I am the Coward in communion
with death

you come to my home of absence

open the night door
trap the mooncast on my walls

you gather your belongings
sour bread
from the graveyard

scent of cremation
sweeps across your face

      mimics the night

light   brushes you
away with the debris

————————

arrogant blood
of day breath

the draping of flesh
to the ground

and children on wings of shadowed light

     the bones of words

and children who bathe the marrow

               a rested mind
               eyes closed

perched in the flame

be fair with my bones
dank   sweat   smell of time
and origin

gardener
by the prayer wall

stream thick in stones

shining rock
that breaks the dark
earth

the standing and the deceased
sweet
shadows on the ridge

————————————

black veils
and wool

rain kneads the earth
unfolding

and a breath
vanishes

your tongue is fire
scattered grain by the road

covet
my branches

annul my breath

there is only asylum
in the turning:

the red attempt of the knife

delusion of
my longest eye   come
                cover me

---

my Dead

sloughed off
in the sand wind

in the coarse sandfalls of dusk light

clear palms
wet to steady the breath talk

a sea thought
        poured
            from the late light

this blessing from the dirt
I have forgiven

stones in my throat
shadows that worry the curving

eyes unnamed in darkness
the falling color and
this step by the door

this resolution of uncarved light
by my fingers

IX

IN THE TEMPORARY MIST OF PRAYER

breath
bowed deep-kneed to the edge of pity
and the summary of prayers

collecting the night
winds
from roses and chamomile weeds
      eyes dead in the frost
      whispers
      from the naked falling

and creation's   dank   smell
a dark quarry of the stranger's winds

prayers
from the split shadows
      cross the name
      that slips
      by the rocks

stones in my throat

ascribe to the soil
the face of god

mouthful
of ascension

    come to these chairs with your feet bound

    seethe
    with the shifting plates of the earth

in sight of censured wind
this ground hollows
your name

———————————

wrapped in swollen greens

you confiscate gray silence
    from the night

breath on your forehead
burning black where blessings recur

an insistence of mercy
in the temporary
mist of prayer

curators for the desert song
for echoes bound by paper
sky
        and specks of swinging
        light

carve sand beetles in the wind

bell-clasp the names of shame of burning white lips
    and cactus blood

circle your neck in dust crumbs   of blue
paper house from the shadows and still lines

sky hawk
a hundred bells in the rain

undetected by the Upper Winds

day of the bluing
and the dead
          silence roams
          in your empty mouth

brush the honeyblood
from unadorned cups

setting stone
the still evening
beats the corners of your eyes

————————————

god of the air and thick leaves

I speak your voice
yellow   breath
of your bones

I appraise the soil
the weak   sea   that drips
disorder
in the morning

the break of being that singes
my lips
in the dirt

fever of a blue slave
glass caress
               of a sky bled by its fir name
by the memory of certainty

          that summons this day in blue knots
in slivers of white birch of porcelain water running through
black

paradigm of breath
you are   An Enraptured Script
reversed light

bent by original black for the turning
of a window lock
                              crashing white
                              inside my mouth

in cream light   you are carved peonies

you speak ivy
shadows out of the brown wind

                                        subtext
                                        in a pounding drum

I am the canal and   the rope
of wood and paint
          obsessed with a windthrown hour
          where night   hides among currents of time

a still field   longing
for morning wreckage

whose fingers
carve bones in thundering
dusk

whose voice is a cave swallow
shadowing the night
bent in a heavy sky

whose echoes
wrapped in knotted breath
string blue
or low rains

for the maddened spinner
of white fire on nightwatch

what is the color of captivity

       hue of centuries
       circling
       at a cell door
              (window bars
              to stay the pressing woods)

       smoke buttressing
       an hour's
       contour
              (range of black
              abiding freefalling white)

or the naked lonely
peeling
paint
as the skin
refracts
a spiraling prism

you are confined to my glass mind
        a soft breaking down
                the sweet mist
                    on my tongue

I am unbearable light
unforgiven

the blue hands
in an illegitimate collaboration

sweet red mask
calm the quiet
calm the woods at my feet
the dark   between my arms

torches in the ravine
        you are roses   dandelions in the rabbit's mouth

stems and thorns
covenants between the insane
        and the gods of deliverance

I am an isolated walk through the silent lens
a dance on the sloping roof

hidden mouth chalked on the sky
in the temper of noon

earth in chance
and the aloneness of breath

X

IS YOUR QUESTION

you hid your face when the whispers began
trills of buried bells and the turning silence
    song wisp

break   break   break   break
an end tone
rescues the dead

and light darts off the lilac branch
ancient storms from the underside of roots
turn the winds tongue
in my mouth

────────────────

among the chrysanthemums
you are singing my name

winding night by a thread
on the spool in your hands

vowels of your holy scream
reverberate in my mouth

burning pages edge my feet

scent of a fall

is this light
yours

a yellow
in bleeds   moon
              turning old

salt shine
through the low moan
of a startled mouth

is your
question
a shadow of sycamores

or an interrupted
pose of rushing
blood

a chant for gathering winter

      voice that turns
      leaves lying
      to wings

you covet the sticks
arranged in my mouth
        the edged and the fields
        that corner memory

and confer with buried temples
of slate
                    with the wheat stalking the night

I loosely confine lilac buds
to the stem
and wear the ending in night
                            spirits

        beggar of the perch
        ancient hum in a breath

inhale
the flame
taste the bird beak on your tongue
without wood
or stone

draw   me   under the darkest dirt

fevered witness
to rivers
burning
to water greens
that elicit the howl

I know your name

I know your body's churning
your held
breath that stakes
a white sky

and with your lips
I drink a brew
of steamed wind
raw

I grieve for your eyes
for the night's white
breath

the river growing
wild
in the absence of a name

your mouth untended
pale horizon
of seasons gone

silence of mingled
words
that bracket the day

———————————

night ruptures in my arms
trembles and flails

I fly to the edge and peer among my dead
cleanse my tongue

here by the river
I sit for you

red wind tiles
are laid

      to collide with the fall

split the ladder rungs

      gathering prayers
      in crossfire   voices melted on the wall

and day begins

———————————

your face is brief

crier
trembling afloat

I recognize you

long forgotten
vowel of the night

we
the unruly and the dead
gather sticks
form acres of swaying hills

steal hinges off iron
doors   whisper
into the morning cup of silence

I fling my hands from the rail

and the hot boil
of air
hums incessantly in my ears

you have mold on your aging eyes

empty pots
fill your balcony

teeth   on a name
extinct

from the tread of the broken step
blackened
wood
an uprooted heaving and whining
        to green and die

a voice that seeps from wind
slender story
                caught
and spun through the haze

tree roots and coffins
berries
underfoot

─────────────────────

lion breath
in the nest

shaking cries
                beneath the rabid roots

Eyes of Semen
bleeding
on fleeing hands

eyes   searching
under the earth

brittle
gold of the waking phrase

when light is just despair

the haze is born
sky creased thick
with moist and dark

loose tails in the grasses
unearthed
        bones of a kill

a memorial to swollen
absence
in the interlude

———————————

closet of wings and patience

whitewashed
bones
        forgiven
        in this light

the religious
and the buried
                tether to the wake of deepening
                red

their uncertainty
steps off the wheel

FREE VERSE EDITIONS

Edited by Jon Thompson

2007

Child in the Road by Cindy Savett
Verge by Morgan Lucas Schuldt
The Flying House by Dawn-Michelle Baude

2006

Physis by Nicolas Pesque, translated by Cole Swensen
Puppet Wardrobe by Daniel Tiffany
These Beautiful Limits by Thomas Lisk
The Wash by Adam Clay

2005

A Map of Faring by Peter Riley
Signs Following by Ger Killeen
Winter Journey [*Viaggio d'inverno*] by Attilio Bertolucci,
   translated by Nicholas Benson

ABOUT THE AUTHOR

Cindy Savett teaches poetry workshops at mental institutions in the Philadelphia area to both acute short-term and residential patients. She has published in numerous print and online journals, including *Margie, Heliotrope, LIT, The Marlboro Review, 26 Magazine, Cutbank,* and *Free Verse.* She is also at work on a memoir on the death of her daughter. Additionally, Cindy has served on several school boards and with other nonprofit agencies. She spent fifteen years in the retail business, traveling extensively overseas. Born and raised in the Philadelphia area, she currently lives in Merion, Pennsylvania, with her husband and children.

Printed in the United States
95483LV00004BA/301-378/A

9 781602 350298